HENRY PURCELL

TE DEUM AND JUBILATE

for St Cecilia's Day 1694
for Solo Voices, Chorus and Orchestra
für Solostimmen, Chor und Orchester
D major/D-Dur/Ré majeur

Edited by/Herausgegeben von
Denis Arnold

Ernst Eulenburg Ltd
London · Mainz · New York · Paris · Tokyo · Zürich

Purcell, Te Deum and Jubilate

St. Cecilia's Day was celebrated in England during Restoration times with a great festival of music. When exactly this custom began is not known, but in 1683, the gentlemen of the Musical Society of London organized a concert held before a large audience in the Stationers Hall. The ode commissioned and composed for this occasion was Purcell's "Welcome to all the Pleasures" (see Eulenburg Edition No. 1062). Usually, the music for the concert was composed to a specially written poem, and it was set for soloists, choir and orchestra. The soloists were among the best singers of the day, and their music was deliberately florid to show their virtuosity.

It is in this tradition that Purcell wrote his festal *Te Deum* and *Jubilate* in D major. It was composed for St. Cecilia's Day, 1694, and shows the same ornate style as the odes composed in previous years. In spite of the fact that most settings of the English liturgy were designed for more modest resources, Purcell gives reign to his most pompous manner. The solo parts are full of graces; the chorus sings massively wrought music; while the orchestra, with its prominent parts for trumpets, reminds us of the composer's dramatic music, where virtuoso display was a vital element in its public appeal. Thus, the *Te Deum* and *Jubilate* are deliciously extrovert and entirely suitable for the greater occasions.

It was this grand manner which assured the popularity of the work. After its initial performance, it was given annually on St. Cecilia's Day for many years. The festivals of the Sons of the Clergy given in St. Paul's Cathedral also provided an opportunity for its performance, and it was heard at these until Handel produced an equally splendid

Der St. Cäcilia-Tag wurde in der Periode der „Restoration" mit festlicher Musik gefeiert. Wir wissen nicht genau, wann dieser Brauch anfing; aber schon 1683 veranstalteten die Mitglieder der Musical Society in London ein Konzert für eine grosse Zuhörerschaft in Stationers Hall. Gewöhnlich wurde die Musik für dieses Konzert zu einem besonders geschriebenen Gedicht komponiert, und wurde für Solisten, Chor und Orchester gesetzt. Die Solisten wurden aus den besten Sängern der Zeit gewählt, und die Musik war absichtlich virtuos gehalten, um ihr Können zu zeigen. Der Komponist des Jahres 1683 war Purcell mit der Ode „Welcome to all the pleasures" (Eulenburg Nr. 1062).

Im Rahmen dieser Tradition schrieb Purcell das festliche *Te Deum* und *Jubilate*. Es wurde für den Cäcilia-Tag 1694 komponiert und zeigt denselben verzierungsreichen Stil wie die Oden der früheren Jahre. Trotzdem die meisten Sätze für die englische Liturgie für bescheidenere Mittel bestimmt waren, lässt Purcell seiner prunkvollen Manier die Zügel schiessen. Die Solostimmen sind voll von Verzierungen; der Chor singt massiv geformte Musik; dagegen erinnert uns das Orchester mit den hervortretenden Trompetenstimmen an die dramatische Musik des Komponisten, bei der die Entfaltung von Virtuosität ein wichtiges Element für öffentliche Anerkennung war. So sind *Tedeum* und *Jubilate* von köstlicher, äusserer Wirkung und durchaus geeignet für besondere Gelegenheiten.

Dieser grosse Stil sicherte dem Werk seine Popularität. Nach der Erstaufführung wurde es viele Jahre lang alljährlich am Cäcilia-Tag aufgeführt. Die Festspiele der Sons of the Clergy, die in St. Pauls Cathedral stattfanden, boten auch eine Gelegenheit für Aufführungen, und das Werk wurde hier gehört, bis Händel im Jahre 1743 eine

setting of the works in 1743. It was also used for the celebrations of victories during the various campaigns of the early 18th century, as the title page of its 2nd edition tells us:

gleich glänzende Vertonung schuf. Es wurde auch benutzt für die Feiern verschiedener Siege in den Kriegen des frühen 18. Jahrhunderts, wie uns die Titelseite der 2. Auflage zeigt:

TE DEUM / ET / JUBILATE / FOR/ VOICES AND INSTRUMENTS/ Perform'd before the / QUEEN, LORDS AND COMMONS, at the / Cathedral-Church of St. Paul / ON THE / THANKSGIVING-DAY / FOR THE / Glorious SUCCESSES of Her MAJESTY'S / Army the last CAMPAIGN / COMPOS'D / By the Late Famous Mr. HENRY PURCELL.

At similar occasions outside London, it was also popular and Mrs. Delany writing from Dublin on November 25th, 1731, describes a concert where it was performed:

Auch bei ähnlichen Gelegenheiten ausserhalb Londons wurde das Werk populär, und Mrs. Delany beschreibt von Dublin aus am 25. November 1731 eine dortige Aufführung.

"Monday being St. Cecilia's Day, it was celebrated with great pomp at St. Patrick's Cathedral. We were there in the greatest crowd I ever saw; we went at ten and stayed till four; there is a very fine organ, which was accompanied by a great many instruments, Dubourg at the head of them; they began with the first concerto of Corelli; we had Purcell's Te Deum and Jubilate; then the fifth concerto of Corelli; after that an anthem of Blow's, and they concluded with the eighth concerto of Corelli . . ."

This fame ensured that the work was printed in score (it was the only church music of Purcell to be available in this form until many years after the composer's death) and it underwent a large number of editions throughout the 18th century.

The present edition has been prepared from the second edition, a copy of which is now in the possession of Glasgow University. This appears to be a reprint of the first edition published under the supervision of Purcell's widow, and although it contains a large number of misprints, there seems to be no reason to doubt its authority as completely as does the editor of Volume 23 of the Purcell Society's collected edition. The misprints are all clearly recognizable, and the main points of doubt are small matters of tied notes and occasional difficulties of verbal underlay. For the rest, it seems unnecessary to make alterations for the sake of uniformity as

Dank dieser Berühmtheit wurde das Werk in Partitur gedruckt (bis lange nach seinem Tode das einzige geistliche Werk von Purcell, das in dieser Form erschien); es erlebte eine grosse Anzahl Auflagen während des 18. Jahrhunderts.

Die vorliegende Ausgabe geht von der 2. Auflage aus, von der sich ein Exemplar im Besitz der Universität Glasgow befindet. Diese war, wie es scheint, ein Abdruck der 1. Ausgabe unter Aufsicht von Purcells Witwe, und obgleich sie eine Menge Druckfehler enthält, besteht kein Grund, ihr jede Authentizität so absolut abzusprechen, wie es der Herausgeber von Bd. 23 der Gesamtausgabe der Purcell-Society tut. Die Druckfehler sind sämtlich leicht erkennbar, und die Hauptpunkte für Zweifel sind Kleinigkeiten, wie gebundene Noten, und gelegentliche Schwierigkeiten der Textunterlegung. Im Übrigen scheint es unnötig, Änderungen im Interesse der Einheitlichkeit zu machen, wie es

has seemingly happened on a number of occasions in the collected edition.

Since the present edition is essentially a practical one, certain points should be noted. The performance of dotted rhythms should be in the French 17th century style, but as double dotting is probably not an exact notation of the note values used, the original notation has been kept, but at certain cadences where it is necessary to double-dot one part to bring it into agreement with others small semiquaver notes have been added above the staves. In the triple time passages the note values have been reduced to one-half those of the original, and 3/2 bars have been inserted to denote *hemiolias*. *Solo* has been substituted for *Verse* and *Chorus* for *Full*. In bars 55 and 57 of the TE DEUM Soprano I and II have been added to the chorus as an obvious reading. Indications in brackets are editorial, otherwise the text is unadulterated.

offenbar gelegentlich in der Gesamtausgabe geschehen ist.

Da die vorliegende Ausgabe hauptsächlich praktischen Zwecken dienen soll, sind folgende Punkte zu berücksichtigen. Punktierte Rhythmen sind im französischen Stil des 17. Jahrhunderts auszuführen; da aber Doppelpunktierung vermutlich nicht den genauen Notenwert wiedergibt, wurde die originale Notierung beibehalten; jedoch wurden dort, wo die Stimmen zusammen fallen müssen, kleine Sechzehntelnoten über den Systemen angebracht. In den dreiteiligen Rhythmen wurden die Notenwerte auf die Hälfte des Originals reduziert, und 3/2-Takte sind eingefügt worden, um die *Hemiolen* zu bezeichnen. *Solo* und *Tutti* wurden für *Verse* und *Full* eingesetzt. In den Takten 55 und 57 des TE DEUM wurden Sopran I und II als selbstverständlich eingefügt. Alle nicht authentischen Angaben sind in Klammern gesetzt; im übrigen wurde der Urtext beibehalten.

DENIS ARNOLD

Te Deum Laudamus in D

Henry Purcell (1659 - 1695)
ed. Denis Arnold

E.E. 6443

E.E. 6443

4

7

E.E. 6443

8

E.E. 6443

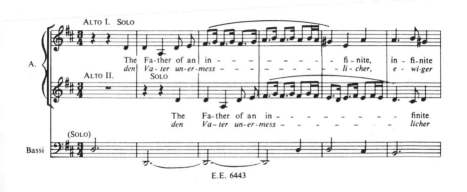

14

E.E. 6443

18

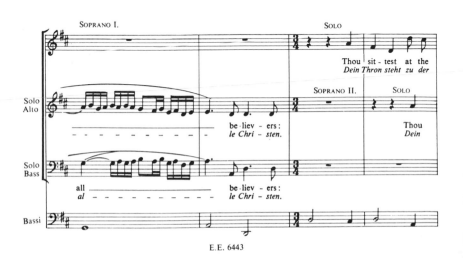

E.E. 6443

23

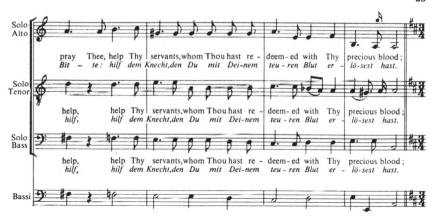

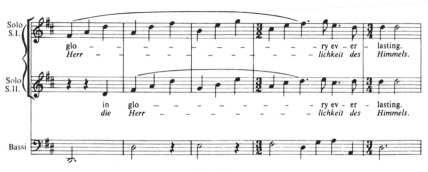

E.E. 6443

28

32

Jubilate Deo in D

Henry Purcell (1659 - 1695)
ed. Denis Arnold

34

E.E. 6143

36

39

E.C. 6443

40

E.E. 6443

E.E. 6443

44

45

E.E. 6443

48

50

E.E. 6443